Making

By Mel Brooke

Thirty-Three Publishing

First Published in Great Britain in 2011 by
Thirty-Three Publishing

ISBN:978-0-9566934-1-9

Printed and bound by CPI Group (UK) Ltd, Croydon, CR0 4YY

All Illustrations by M. Brooke

All text and photographs by M.Brooke

Contents

About the Author

Mel Brooke has been crafting in some shape or form all her life and what started out as an obsession for crocheting granny squares has led her to happily dance her way through life knitting, sewing, mosaic-ing, embroidering, beading and having fun with a whole batch of other crafts too numerous to mention.
'After all', she says 'why stop at one?'

This is Mel's second book - the first being a book of colourful beading projects titled 'Lili's Funky Beading Book' (published 2010). She also runs an online retail website that sells beads (www.BeadsbyLili.com), has had many projects in beading and craft magazines and makes films for 'BeadClub' channel on You Tube. In her spare time she is, of course, always busy and addicted to making stuff!

Introduction

As a child I grew up amongst a generation of 'ladies-who-craft' and, it seems, it is one of the main influences that has stayed with me into my adult life. Some of my earliest memories are of excitedly leaving one of my dolls with my Grandmother, only to get it back a week or so later with a whole new outfit of clothes all perfectly sewn by hand and always the envy of my friends who asked if their dolls could go for a visit too!

In addition to the Dolls, Pyjama Cases, Bags and other handmade works of art that came my way was the utter excitement of being allowed to look in the button tin, play with fabrics or browse the box of tangled embroidery threads in an array of delicious rainbow colours. How could you not be affected by this treasure trove of textiles, colours and patterns? How could you not want to play!

In fairness to my Grandmother, I believe her introduction to crafting probably came from necessity, such was the reality of having to 'make do & mend' during the hardships of WWII with a family of 5 children to feed & clothe on the barest of budgets. Of course, the skills were passed on to the children too and I have heard many stories from my mother and her sisters about how they would re-fashion new clothes from old and make jewellery from buttons and wire as they grew up in austere times.

My Mother also continued to make things - including her own & our clothes for years but to be honest I don't think I always appreciated her efforts, wanting as you do, the latest fashions from trendy high street shops like Chelsea Girl & Top Shop during an era when affordable fashion came into the picture. Thankfully it didn't put her off and instead I have received many pretty aprons, peg bags and other thoughtful little gifts through the years - each one a labour of love and, truth be known, driven by an inbuilt obsession to create! There is also no doubt in my mind that, as well as being addictive, crafting has a therapeutic purpose - both physical and mental which again adds to its enduring popularity.

Now, with the trend for 'making and doing' there is a whole new generation of crafters who are keen to get stuck in and that is really where this book comes in - inside you will find an eclectic mix of projects for you to try. Many are a modern take on retro craft projects and some are just for fun because I believe not everything has to have a purpose other than that lovely feeling of satisfaction you get from simply.... making..... something.....

Raffia Wrapped Bangle

Fashion colours and trends change so fast each season and most girls will find they have an out of date colour bangle or two hiding in the back of their jewellery box. Well, this is a great way to re-cycle those forgotten pieces and give them a whole new look. Any colour raffia can be used to bring your bangles up to date and you can change it again next season which makes this a real eco project!

Tools & Materials: Scissors, Wool Needle, Plain Bangle, Natural Raffia, 4mm Beads

Pull out some strips of raffia from the bunch ready to work with, then olding a 4-5cm end against the inside of the bangle, begin to wrap it round. Thread the working end through its own loop before it pulling ght to the bangle. Continue to work your way around the bangle with trips of raffia.

very time you have to add a new piece, leave an end from the revious piece that is just long enough to be wrapped over and 'hidden' y the new piece.

When you have wound the raffia strands all the way around the bangle, back to the beginning, wrap and cover the first end over as neatly as you can. Trim and tuck the final end in underneath one of the wrapped strands on the inside of the bangle.
At this point you could add a very tiny dot of glue underneath the raffia to secure it.

ext, use a needle and thread to add a few beads to the outside f the bangle. If working the beads into small groups (as shown) ush the needle under the raffia threads between attaching them o that the running thread doesn't show.

ry to tie any knots under the bead clusters so that once you have immed the thread they won't be visible.

Top Tip: *Try wrapping with ribbon or thin strips of fabric to give the bangle a different textile feel*

Butterfly Flutterby Brooch

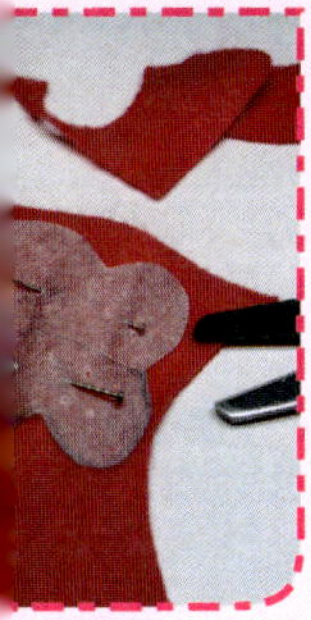

Who can resist a crafty flutter with a Butterfly? Not me that's for sure! Hopefully once you've made one of these you will be inspired to make your own colour variations of this cute brooch project. They would make lovely little gifts and could be pinned on bags, lapels or hats... whatever takes your fancy!

Tools & Materials: Felt, Net Fabric, Scissors, Needle & Thread, Seed Beads, Brooch Finding

Use the pattern in the back of the book to cut out the following:

1 x Small Butterfly
1 x Large Butterfly (different colour of felt)
5 x Large Butterfly shapes in netting.

Layer 3 of the net butterfly shapes and make a running stitch up the center. Pull the end of the thread so that the net butterflies 'ruche' slightly then sew them onto the larger felt butterfly.

Sew seed beads onto the smaller felt butterfly, making sure to have a central row to give the butterfly a beady 'body'. Add lots to fill in the wings and then sew a row of little beads around the edge of the larger felt butterfly too.

Sew the small beaded butterfly directly onto the top of the ruched net butterfly layers.

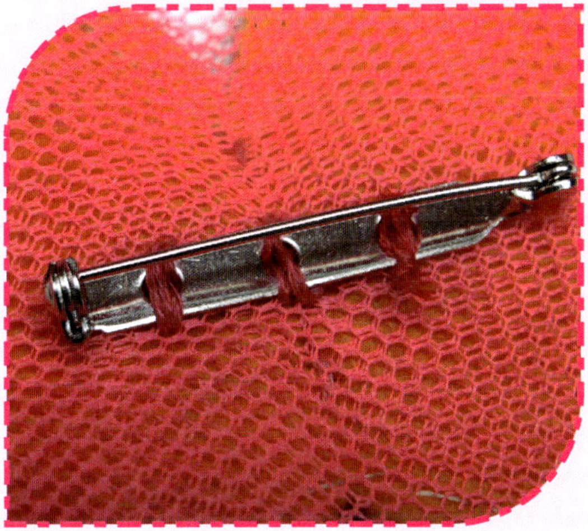

Hold the last 2 pieces of net butterfly shapes together and sew them onto the back of the large felt butterfly.

Use a thicker embroidery thread to attach the brooch back finding to the back of the butterfly.

Top Tip: *If you don't have a brooch finding simply use a large safety pin!*

Patchwork String of Hearts

There's something lovely about a string of hearts with little words stuck in their centres. These shabby chic style cuties are created from nothing more than waste packaging, magazine pages and glue using a basic but effective crafting technique called 'Decoupage'. Be warned though... it's another of those simple but addictive pursuits that will have you covering all sorts of things!

Tools & Materials: Scissors, Cardboard, Magazine Pages & PVA Glue

tart by drawing three different size hearts onto some cardboard (scrap ardboard from cereal boxes or such is just fine!).

lext, choose some pages from an old magazine or supplement that has retty floral fabric prints on it and cut some little strips from it. The strips an vary in thickness and length - in fact the more random the better the nd effect.

Paste some PVA glue onto the front of the first heart and begin to add little strips of paper. Overlap them a little and carefully fold over the edges, adding more glue with your fingers to help smooth them around the shaped sides. Leave it to dry before turning over and filling in the gaps on the back.

When the back is dry turn it back over and give the front another thick coating of PVA. Dry and repeat on the back.

Cover the remaining two cardboard hearts in the same way as the first - giving each that extra last layering of glue to act as a varnish.

ut three individual words from magazine headlines or text and position them onto ach heart. Glue them in place and then cover with another layer of PVA.

ut a 1mtr length of raffia or cord and double it. Stick the middle and each side to he back of the smallest heart with sticky tape. Leave a gap of around 6 cm before ticking the threads to the back of the middle size heart, then repeat again on the argest heart. Tie threads into a bow to finish.

Top Tip: *Try covering the hearts in words or letters that make up a special message or name !*

Floral Bow Hair Band

This is another great little project for customising something you might otherwise throw away. This time it's a plastic hairband covered in cute floral fabric and given a little side bow. Whilst this version is quite summery you could use the same technique to cover a band with satin fabric for a bridesmaid, wedding guest or party girl style!

Tools & Materials: Scissors, Needle & Cotton, Fabric, Plastic Hair Band, PVA Glue

tart by cutting several long strips of fabric that are approx. 2cm wide. se glue to attach the fabric to one end of the hair band and a bull dog clip hold the end in place while it dries. Then wrap the strip all the way round the band, neatly folding over one edge as you work to cover the ugh edge and using more dots of glue to help hold the fabric in place.

Cut a 7cm x 24cm fabric rectangle. Press the two long edges to the center, slightly overlapping, and dot some glue to hold them in place. Next, bring the ends to the middle and dot with glue to hold them in place. Trim off any loose threads to neaten up.

Fold the middle of the bow like a fan and hold it in place with a pin. Take a needle and cotton and sew through the sides a couple of times so that the bow holds its shape.

ut a small rectangle of fabric that measures 4cm x 5cm. Fold the des into the middle as before then use it to wrap around the enter of the bow.

titch the ends underneath, attaching it to the fabric wrapped and at the same time.

Top Tip: *Try wrapping your hairband with several strands of ribbon for a multi-layered effect!*

Funky Felt Case

Often with summer sunglasses of the not-so-expensive variety you will get a cheap nylon drawstring case that doesn't really provide much protection. Felt is softer, thicker and will provide much better protection for glasses when not being worn. It is also easy to decorate and personalize which is really what this little project is all about....

Tools & Materials: Scissors, Felt, Wool & Needle, Embroidery Threads & Needle.

ut out 2 x rectangles of felt that measure as follows:

(1) 9cm wide by 23cm long
(2) 9cm wide by 19cm long

*(*double check to make sure this will fit your sunglasses!)*

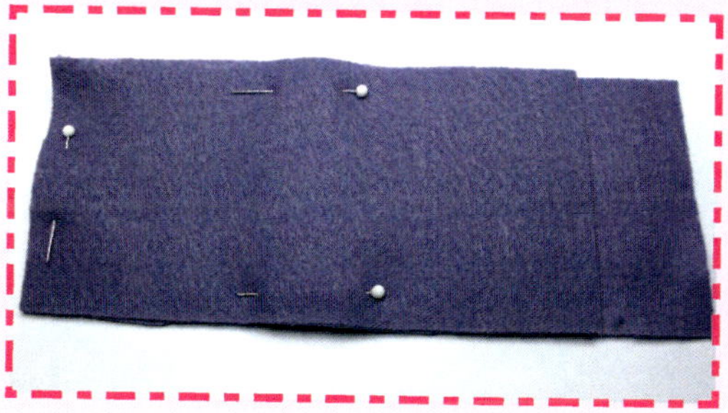

Trace the little guitar pattern in the back of this book then use it to cut out the in a complimentary colour felt piece. Use colourful embroidery threads to embellish the guitar with swirling patterns and tiny stitches.

Layer the smaller felt rectangle on top the large rectangle, and pin the ends together followed by the sides. Fold the top over & re-check the fit for your glasses.

osition the embroidered guitar shape and sew it into place. Use a different contrasting colour thread to ew on your name or more decorative patterns (simple back stitch is easiest). Blanket stitch around the ree sides of felt to attach together then blanket stitch along the 'flap' and add a button with a popper or elcro dot underneath.

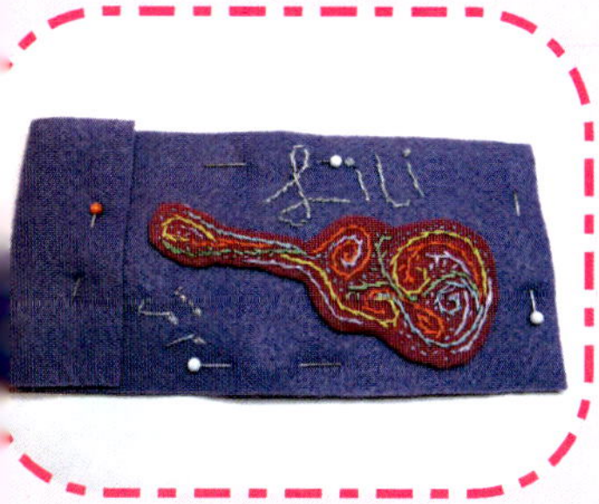

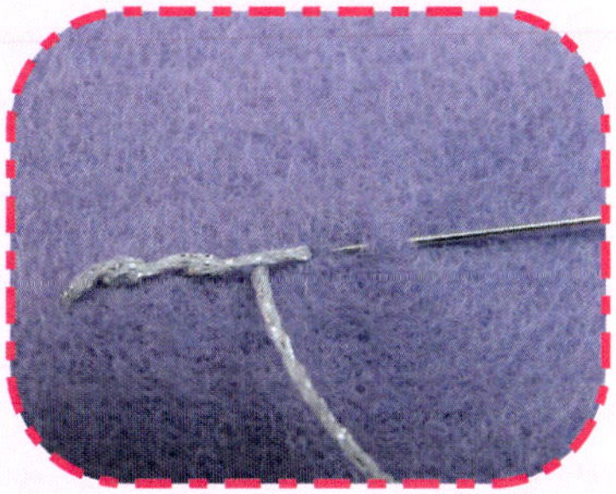

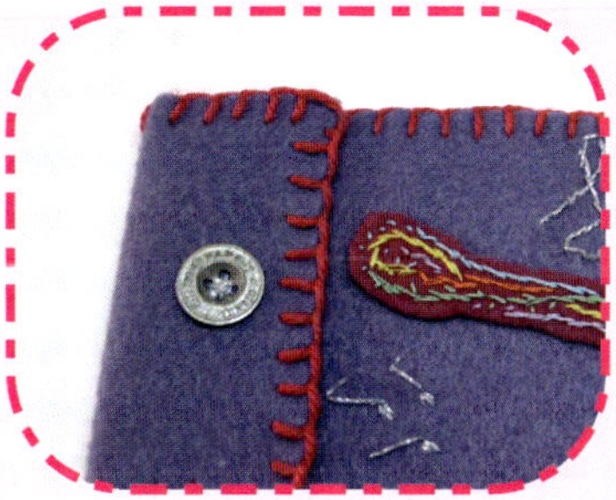

Top Tip: This same basic design could be adjusted to accommodate a mobile phone!

Lazy Daisy Flower Bunting

Here's a different take on the ever popular bunting! It looks great in the garden or indoors and made of bright faux raffia colours like this one it will not only be eye-catching & totally gorgeous but I'm willing to bet you will be inundated with requests to make more!

Tools & Materials: Scissors, Flower Loom, Synthetic Raffia, Sticky Tape, Wool Needle/Bodkin

Begin by making a knot in the end of a strand of raffia so that you can slide into the slit on the side of the flower loom to hold it in place. Wrap the raffia ack and forth across the flower loom in a 'figure of 8'.

ontinue until you have been all the way around and back to the beginning. rim the end of the raffia and use sticky tape to secure it to the side of the om.

Thread a contrasting piece of raffia onto your wool needle (or bodkin) and, starting from the underneath of the flower, sew up and down through the gaps in the raffia 'petals'. Sewing back and forth across the center will give you a pretty 'star' shape to the middle of your flower.

Finish off by knotting the strands together a couple of times and trimming the ends.

/hen you have made 12-15 flowers they are ready to start :ringing. Attach them to one long strand of raffia by looping rough a top 'petal' on each flower then leaving a gap before ɔu add the next one.

ake a loop on each end so that the bunting can be pinned r hung up in a location of your choosing!

Top Tip: *Use the same basic flower loom technique to make pretty fabric or ribbon flower bunting!*

Bejewelled Flip Flops

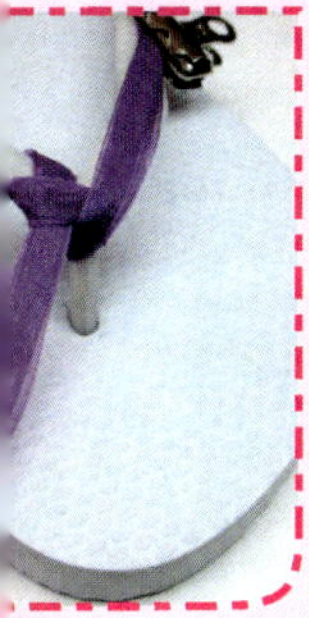

We all have the odd summer sandal lurking that is not exactly exciting so this 'customising' project is a great challenge to funk up the flip flops - who'd guess what a bit of ribbon, a few beads and a teaspoon could achieve!

Tools & Materials: Flip Flops, 5mtrs Organza Ribbon, Scissors, Needle, Clear Nylon Thread, Glue

Double the ribbon twice then wrap the middle of it around the toe 'stem' in the middle of the flip flop. Working on the first side, loop the ends of ribbon through itself to secure it. It helps to clip the other side out of the way for a minute.

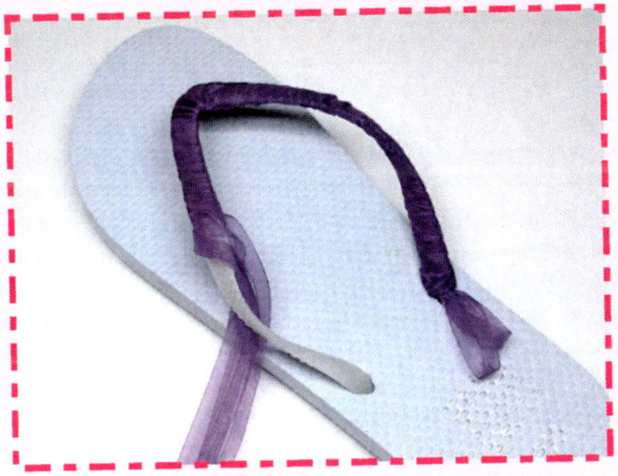

Next, wrap the ribbon all the way around the flip flop band, trying to keep it neat and with a slight overlap as you work. When you reach the end, tuck the tail ends through itself again and pull quite tight.

Repeat the wrapping process on the second side of the flip flop.

Take a needle threaded with strong nylon and begin to attach beads to the ribbon by sewing them to layers of wrapped ribbon. If you need to add more thread as you work, hide the knots under the ribbon layers or beads so that they are not visible.

To finish off, trim the ends of ribbon on either side and use the end of a teaspoon to push them neatly down into the base of the flip flop arms (you can add a tiny dot of glue into the base of each arm to secure them if desired).

Top Tip: *Use a thimble to protect your fingers tips when sewing!*

T-Shirt Monster Madness

My son's reaction to this 'Monster' was a beaming grin from side to side of his face when he 'met' it for the first time! Kids grow out of clothes fast and sometimes they are just not good enough to give away so this project is a great way to recycle them and just might give you the inspiration to make more fun keepsakes from a favourite 'T'.

Tools & Materials: Scissors, Needle & Cotton, Wool Needle, 1 x Old T-Shirt, 2 x Buttons, Wool, Soft Toy Filling

Jse scissors to remove the bottom half of the t-shirt from underarm to ıderarm. Cut the large piece of fabric in two. Take the first half and turn side out and sew around the three edges, leaving just a small enough ap on one side to be able to turn it right way round again.

ently stuff the pillow shape with soft toy filling until it is full then fold the dges of the gap neatly inward and sew them together with a running stitch ɔ that most of the stitching doesn't show. Plump it up to even out the uffing then pull the top corners up and push the middle down so that it creates the 'ear' shapes.

Cut x 2 arm/hand shapes from the remaining half of the t-shirt fabric, turn them back to back and sew around the edges, leaving enough of a gap at the 'arm' ends to be able to turn them right way round again.

Now stuff the arms as before, folding the edges of the gaps inward and sewing them together with a running stitch. Position one on either side of the 'pillow' and sew into place.

ut 2 x different size rectangles of coloured felt, making sure the larger ıe is big enough to sit under the buttons. Sew the buttons onto the rge piece of felt with wool to create the eyes. Thread some wool onto large needle and use it to blanket stitch around the felt rectangle and ɔld the eyes piece in place. Sew a 'teeth' pattern onto the smaller felt ɛctangle with wool then use a needle and thread to sew it onto e 'Monster'.

Top Tip: Design different features for the face or maybe sew on some wool 'hair'!

Magical Lavender Star

There's something lovely and calming about working with lavender stems and when it's ready to be harvested from the garden it seems a shame to just pull off the heads to stuff little bags! This little project uses whole flower stems to create a scented star that you can hang long after the summer scents have drifted away.....

Tools & Materials: Scissors, Waxed Cord, 18 x Lavender Flower Stems, 20cm x 3mm Checked Ribbon

rim all the Lavender stems to the same length then group into three's. Take vo bunches and cross them over each other just underneath the flower heads.

ut a long strand of waxed cord and use it to bind the stems together over the ossed parts.

/ind the rest of the cord along the stems of one bunch all the way to the other nd leaving gaps of 5-10mm between each wind of the cord. Try to keep the ension of the cord even as you wind it.

Place a third bunch of stems over the bottom of the group that you have just wrapped with cord. Wrap them where they cross as before. Cross the bunch back over the first bunch to create a triangle shape and continue wrapping cord around the stems and crossed stems until you are back to where you started. Knot the cord to fasten off and trim the ends

lake a second triangle of Lavender stems as above then lay one over e top of the other to create a star shape. Use more cord to bind the roups of stems together where they cross so that the star holds s shape.

inally tie a bow with the ribbon on to decorate & add a cord loop at the ack so that you can hang it up.

Top Tip: If you have a really good crop of Lavender use more stems per small bunch to make a thicker star!

Rag Rug Mug Cosy

If like me you are always making a cuppa and then getting distracted so that your tea goes cold then this might be just the thing! It's a cool 'n' fluffy mug cosy that can be made from coloured hessian (or old sacking if you have it) and then 'rag rugged' with old materials such as the pieces of denim in this version.

Tools & Materials: Scissors, Wool & Needle, Rag Rug Tool, Hessian, Denim scraps.

o begin with cut a rectangle of hessian that fits around your chosen mug, om one side of the handle to the other which should leave the smallest ap in between. Blanket stitch around all the edges with wool.

ut lots of strips of denim that measure approximately 1cm x 6cm. Pull em through your fingers to give them frayed edges. Starting in one orner of the hessian, push the nose of the rag rug tool through a loop and en open the nose so that you can grip one of the denim strips in it.

Pull the denim back through the loop to half way and then pull the ends up each side of the loop. Repeat to add the next strip of denim a few loops along from the first piece. Keep working over the whole of the piece of hessian until you have filled it and then go back to fill any gaps you may have left.

To create the 'clasp', sew a large bead or button onto one end of the rectangle of hessian.

n the opposite side, use the wool to make a loop that fits over the ead and is short enough to hold the two sides of the mug cosy gether when it's closed around the mug.

emember to put the mug cosy on the mug before you make your rink so that you don't spill your drink trying to do it after!

Top Tip: *Old t-shirt material or wool make great variations to work with !*

Festival
Wrap Bracelet

I love making these simple wrap style bracelets - they are so easy! As long as you can make a plait then you can make this bracelet and you need no tools other than scissors with which to make them! There are so many pretty charms and threads available nowadays that once you've mastered this technique you will want to experiment with lots of different varieties!

Tools & Materials: Scissors, Waxed Cord, 1 x 14mm Acrylic Bead & Colourful Acrylic Peace Charms.

Begin by cutting 3 x 3mtr lengths of waxed cord. Hold them all together nd double them. Hold the middle of the threads with your fingers and tie n overhand knot to make a loop on the end. Before you tighten the knot, ake sure that the loop is big enough to fit over the 14mm acrylic bead.

ecure the loop to your work surface with tape or a pin so that it won't ip around as you make the bracelet.

Separate out the strands in to pairs underneath the knot. Begin to plait the cords then after 1cm or so, take one of the pairs of cords on one side of the plait and separate them out. Thread one of the charms directly onto a single strand of the cord. Slide it down to the plait, hold the two cords together again and continue to plait all three. After 1-2cm separate out threads on the opposite side and add another charm as before. Continue until the plait is long enough to wrap around your wrist a couple of times.

/hen the plait is long enough, twist all the ends of cord together and thread on ie 14mm acrylic bead. Slide the bead up to the bottom of the plait and tie a ιot underneath it. Try to make sure the knot sits snugly underneath the bead.

rim the cord ends and to wear, wrap around your wrist a couple of times and ick the bead under the loop!

Top Tip: *Sit shorter cord ends in the middle of the longer ends to pull through.*

Miss Linzi Dollface

1

It can be useful to have a weighted back door stop to help stop the back door slamming in the breeze. This is a modern take on the 'Dolly Door Stops' made by my Grandmother & Mother - except this one is a rather Gothic looking madam which we have nicknamed 'Linzi Dollface' after one of my daughter's flame haired friends!

Tools & Materials: Curvy Plastic Bottle, Sand, Calico, Fabric, Toy Stuffing, Scissors, Needle & Threads

2

he best bottles for this project are the 'curvy' plastic drink bottles that look like ready made bust & torso! Wash out the bottle then fill it to the brim with sand) and screw the cap back on. Seal around the cap with sticky tape.

ut a saucer size circle of calico and roughly position over the bottle cap so that you can roughly pencil where the face features will sit.

Embroider the eyes, nose and mouth (2) or stick on pieces of shaped felt if you are not confident with stitches. Position the circle back over the top of the bottle and stick the bottom of it to the bottle with sticky tape. Stick the back of the circle to the other side then push the toy filling in from each side to create more of a 'head' shape (3). Stick the sides down and run some stitches around the 'neck' to secure the edges in place.

o make the hair, cut a long length of wool and double it. Cut lots of shorter strands and attach them to the ouble strand with larks head knots (4). Tie it around the cap at the top of the bottle then sweep some of e wool strands back over the top to cover it. Cut out 2 x arm shapes, sew around the edges, turn inside ut and stuff them. Wrap fabric around the tops to create 'sleeves (5) then tuck in the ends and sew eatly. Wrap the 'body' of the bottle in fabric and stick or sew at the back to hold in place. Position and ew an arm onto each side of the bottle (6) Have fun accessorizing the doll by putting ribbons in her hair nd making miniature necklaces & bracelets

4

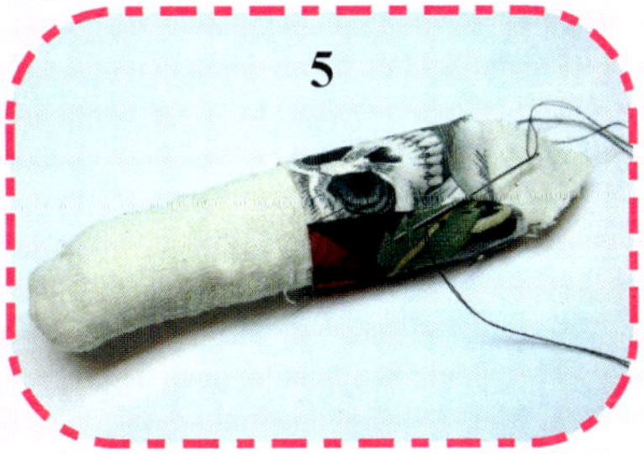
5

6

Top Tip: *Make up your own character dolls by changing the clothing & hair styles!*

Terracotta
Mosaic Heart

What's not to love about hearts? This little air dry terracotta colour clay beauty needs no kiln and is a great way of recycling that pretty piece of broken china or glass. If you want to get real fancy you could even scent it with essential oil before it dries!

Tools & Materials: Air Dry Clay, Broken china, Hammer/Nippers, Drinking Straw, Nail File, Ribbon

Place your china between a couple of sheets of old newspaper and break up into small pieces using a hammer or tile nippers.

Next, roll out your clay to slightly thicker than the pieces of china and cut a heart shape in it. If the surface is marked, dip your finger into a little water and gently smooth over the top of the clay.

Decide where you would like the hanging hole to be positioned and use a short length of ordinary drinking straw to make the hole.

Select small pieces of broken up china and very gently push it into the surface of the clay heart. Do not push too quick or too hard because you will distort the shape of the heart too much.

As you push in the pieces of china, keep check on the shape of the heart and gently re-shape as necessary.

Leave the heart to dry out for 24hrs or so. When it is fully dry you can use an ordinary nail file or fine sandpaper to smooth the edges if needed.

Finally cut a short length of ribbon, thread it through the hole and knot ready to hang.

Top Tip: *If the china pieces fall out when the clay is dry just use craft glue to stick them back in*

Coiled
Paper Treasures

I think Quilling is almost a forgotten art and yet it is something that can not only create beautiful patterns and images for cards but can also be used to create 'paper jewels' such as this. Once you get to grips with making the coils you can squeeze them into all sorts of shapes and glue together to make freestanding 3D pieces for all sorts of homewares and accessories!

Tools & Materials: Scissors, Paper Trimmer, Cocktail Stick, Magazine Pages, PVA Glue

elect a colourful magazine page (full page fashion adverts are usually best!) .en trim width ways into thin strips. A paper trimmer or shredder will give etter uniformity than strips cut with scissors.

old the end of a strip onto a cocktail stick with your fingers then roll the paper ghtly around it, trying to keep all the edges together in a neat roll. Slide it off e cocktail stick letting it loosen slightly.

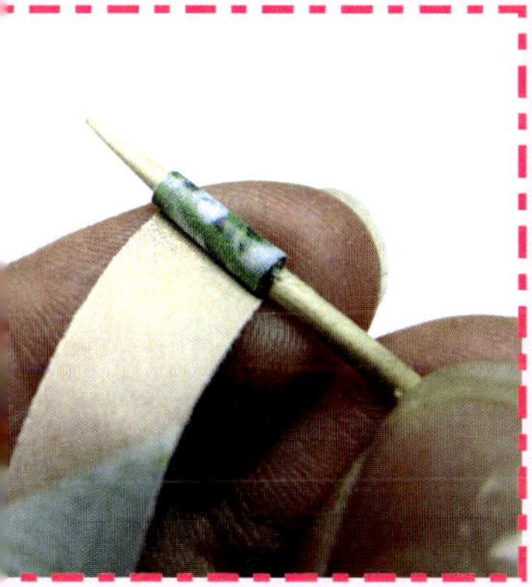

For smaller coils do not loosen too much and dab some glue on the end to secure the coil shape. For larger coils, let the paper roll uncurl slightly before sticking down the end. Leave the coils to dry for a while. To make a teardrop shape simply squeeze one end of a coil. To make a 'leaf' shape, squeeze both ends as shown below.

Arrange your coils together on a flat, non-stick surface to make the basic pattern or shape of your design. Using different colour coils and shapes will give better distinction on the design i.e. use green coils for leaf shapes and pinks or reds for petals.

s a good idea to coat each side of the pieces in water thinned PVA to give it a arnish' like protection but you have to very delicately brush it on to your eces or the coils may 'clump'!

nce your quilled pieces are fully dry they can be strung onto ribbon to make retty pendants, have a pin glued on the back for a simple brooch or attach to arring findings by slipping a jump ring through a coil to link them.

Top Tip: *Paste a magazine page with PVA & leave to dry before cutting into strips for longer lasting coils*

Funky Flower Power Bag

There are so many great value jute shopping bags around at the moment as an eco alternative to plastic carriers that I decided to customise one with a festival of colourful crochet flowers! These are so simple - even if you have never picked up a crochet hook and once you get started you wont want to stop making them !

1

Tools & Materials: 4.5 Crochet Hook, Wool, Needle & Scissors

he flowers start with a basic chain stitch that is created using two strands of contrasting colour wool. ake a slip knot and slide the loop onto the crochet hook (1).

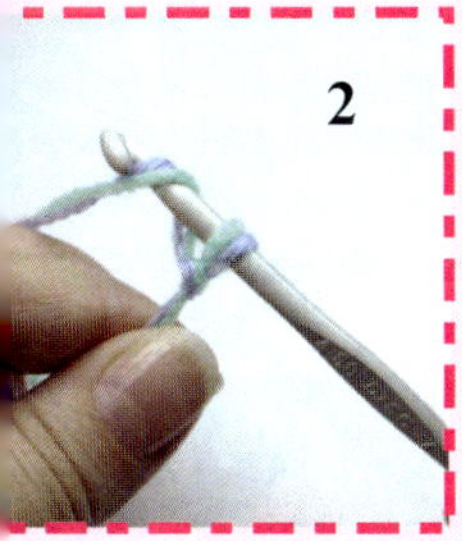

2

Hold the strands underneath the knot and wind the wool around the crochet hook once (2). Use the hook to pull the wool down through the loop and out the other side (3). Slide the loop along the crochet hook and repeat steps 2 & 3 until you have a row of 5 chain stitches (4).

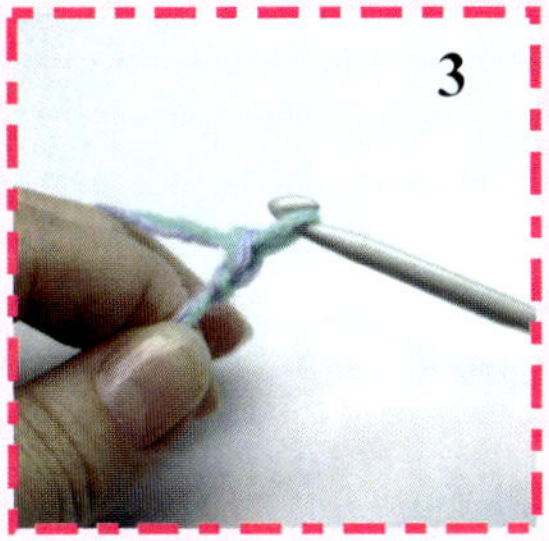

3

4

ush the hook through the first chain stitch and wind the wool around it (5). Pull the wool back through the op as before so that you have created a circle with your chain stitches (6). Make 10 new chain stitches n top of the stitch on the hook (7).

eeping the row of chain at the front of the circle, put the hook through the center, wind the wool around it om the back and pull it all the way back through the circle and the loop on the crochet hook. Now you will ave your first 'petal'. Repeat the steps to make 7 more petals but on the last one, cut the wool and pull it l the way through the loop on the crochet hook to fasten off. Make lots of flowers and sew them onto the hopping bag with big colourful buttons in the middle of each one.

5

6

7

8

Top Tip: If your flowers don't quite cover up the logo simply sew a piece of hessian underneath

Dipsy Daisy Ring

1

This handmade waxed cord flower ring is cuter than cute and there is not a bit of metal in sight! It's feminine and pretty and could be made in wool or ribbon just as easily - just see how many variations you will want to make once you've got the basics mastered!

Tools & Materials: 4mm Knitting Needles, 0.6mm Waxed Cord (Blue & Cream), Flower Loom, Wool Needle & Scissors

1ake a small flower with some blue cord (1), using the basic loom technique shown for the Flower unting (p.16) Leave the center strands of cord quite long at the back and put it to one side.

2

(2) Make a slip knot and slide the loop onto a knitting needle
(3) Push the second knitting needle through the bottom of the loop.
(4) Bring the thread from the back over the top of the second needle

3

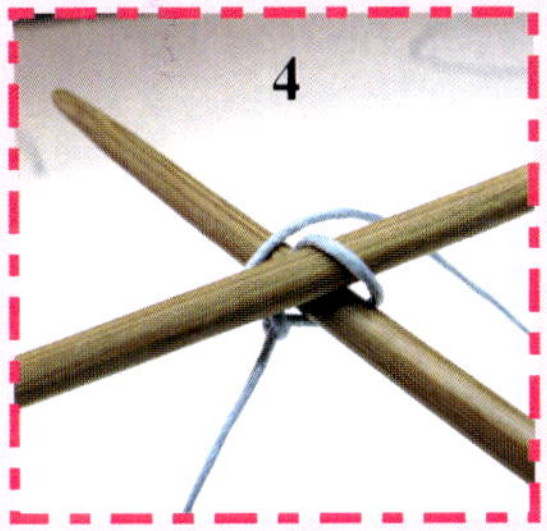
4

;) Draw the second needle back through the loop, making sure to 'catch' the thread so it creates a loop.
;) Slide the loop back onto the first needle and pull the thread to tighten the loop (so that you end up ith two stitches on the needle)
') Repeat steps 3-6 until you have 12 stitches 'cast' on the needle. Then repeat steps 3-5 but instead ' adding the stitch to the first needle, slip it onto the second needle to make the first knitted stitch. epeat until all stitches are on the second needle. Swap the needles around and repeat to make the ext knitted row.
;) After 4 rows 'cast off' by knitting the first two stitches then bringing the first stitch over the top of the econd. Repeat until all stitches are off the needle and use the cord to 'sew' up the two ends & add the ower to hide the join.

5

6

7

8

Top Tip: *To make a larger ring just increase the number of stitches when you cast on*

cheeky

Charming Robots

Keep yourself (or the kids) amused for hours drawing and designing robots to make into charms. Even the worst artists will find that their creations look totally cute once shrunk to a 7th of their size! The charms can be used to make a bracelet or all sorts of other jewellery items and of course you don't have to stick to robots - it could be aliens... monsters... shoes....cupcakes... whatever you love!

Tools & Materials: Scissors, Heat Gun, Shrink Plastic Sheets, Tweezers, Jewellery findings (optional)

Draw or print some little robots onto the sheet of shrink plastic then colour em in lightly with coloured pencils - there's no need to colour in thickly s the pencil colours intensify once you heat the plastic.

ut around the robots, leaving an edge of 2-3mm around the picture. Use hole punch to make a hole in the top of the shape so it can be used to onnect the charm later.

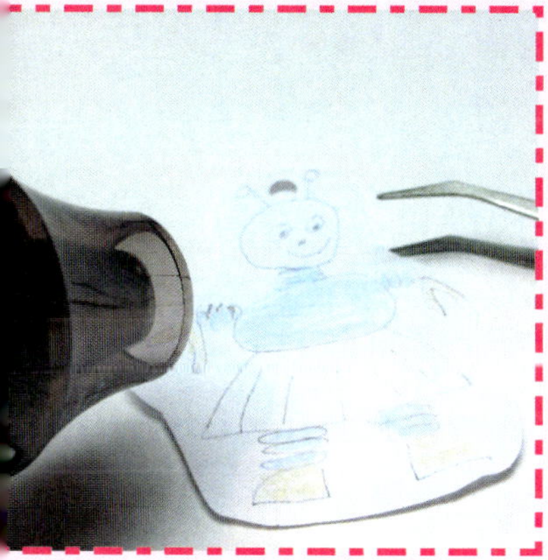

Place the charms on a tray and bake as per the manufacturers instructions or, if you have a heat gun place the charms on a heat proof surface, hold the heat gun over the top of the plastic shape and blast with heat!

Tweezers are great at helping to catch the plastic which will be rolling around a lot and shrivelling under the heat. For both methods, the charms are ready when the plastic stops curling and flattens back out. Make sure to pick it up with tweezers - not fingers as the plastic needs to cool down!

ake or heat all the cut outs so you have a nice batch of little harms to use in your craft projects..

you want to put the charms onto an item of jewellery simply open ome 5-6mm jump rings and slide through the holes on the tops of e charms. Attach directly to the jump rings on a stretchy charm racelet blank or earring finding.

Top Tip: *Make some extra beaded charms to hang between your plastic charms or make a keyring!*

All 'in a row....

Pretty Maids

These mini-madams will hold your make up brushes, favourite pens, nail files or simply just look cute on your dressing table - they are very boudoir! If you want to take it a step further you could make them little 2D felt heads but I'll leave that up to you.... after all, with this project much of the fun is in the design variations!

Tools & Materials: Scissors, Yogurt Drink Bottles, Felt/Fabric, Needle, Pins & Cotton

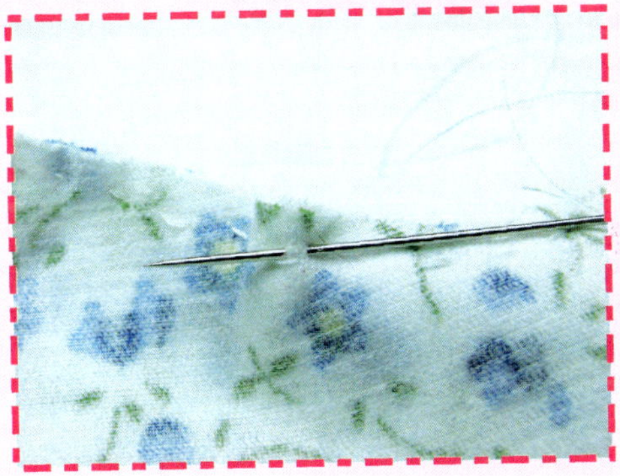

Wash well and dry out an old yogurt drink bottle first - these are the best ıape bottles to use as they already have a nice curvy shape

hoose your fabric and cut out the corset pieces from the pattern page at the ack of the book. Sew the back and sides together but leave the front open.

using felt there's no need to hem the front panels but you may want to with otton fabrics. If using fabric you may need to sew a 5-10mm hem for best fit.

Check the bodice fit around the bottle - it helps to pin it directly to into the plastic. Make any necessary fitting adjustments if the seams need it.

If using felt you can punch holes up both sides of the front panels with something sharp such as a skewer. Then you can thread ribbon or cord directly through the holes to lace it up.

Alternatively you can make little stitches with embroidery threads to make it look like buckles or sew simple 'cross' stitches all the way up to make it look like the bodice has been laced.

inally, to cover the neck end of the bottle either thread some little beads nto elastic thread or cut a strip of netting and run a thread through it before athering it up to make a 'frill'.

se ribbon, decorated felt strips and many other materials to pretty ɔ your maids - just let your imagination have a play!

Top Tip: *Pop some sand or coins in the bottom to give the bottles some weight*

chunky

Clay Buttons

Air dry clay is a wonderfully versatile craft medium and . as it says on the tin. it needs no kiln or cooking! These simple buttons are a great way to try it out as they need very little shaping and you can try out a variety of paint and coating techniques without wasting too much. Big buttons such as these will also look fab on your chunky winter knits or strung together to make bold bracelets!

Tools & Materials: Air Dry Clay, Skewer, Emery Board, Acrylic Paint, Varnish or PVA Glue

tart out by laying a couple of 'guides' ,such as rulers or pieces of wood, either de of your clay as you roll it out on your work surface so that is of even thickness. se a small round shape cutter to cut out the buttons and squeeze all the excess ay together to use later but keep covered with a damp cloth or put it in a sealed ag to stop it drying out. Dab your finger lightly in some water then smooth over the p, bottom and sides of the beads. Before they dry out, use a wooden skewer to ush through the button to make the holes for threading. Leave to dry thoroughly vernight is best) - turning from time to time so that both sides get the air.

When the buttons are dry, use an emery board to carefully rub the side and backs of the holes to remove the rough edges. Turn the buttons on their fronts and paint the backs and sides first - allow to dry before turning over to paint the fronts.

You can use a variety of painting techniques to decorate them such as dipping, sponging, ragging or decorating by hand with a paint brush.

eave the painted buttons to dry very thoroughly or else you risk ining the effect when you coat with varnish or watered PVA.

/hen the buttons are dry you may need to re-clear the threading oles before use if they have become clogged with varnish or paint.

Top Tip: Roll the clay out on hessian for a more textured bead surface!

I've got a... Crush-on-Shoe Mobile

Sometimes you just have to make random objects that feature those things that make you happy ... the ones you have a little crush on! In this case it's shoes - so here's a colour poppin' mobile strung with little plastic high heel shoes which dangle and twirl from beaded strands!

Tools & Materials: Scissors, Waxed Cord, Bag Handle (Hoop Shape), Mixed Beads & Shoe Charms.

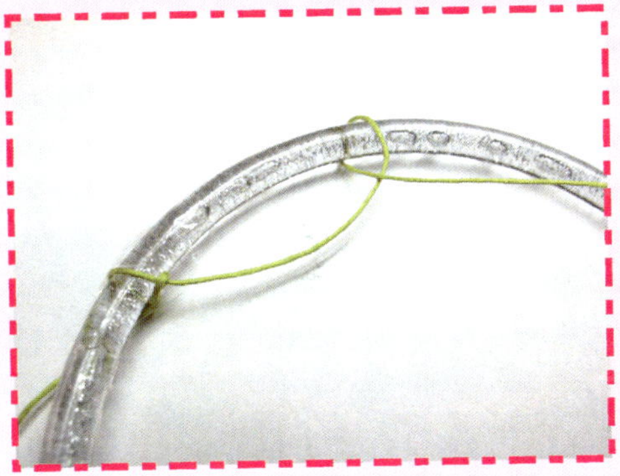

Attach a long piece of waxed cord to the bag handle hoop. It helps to use icky tape to secure the knot and stop it sliding about as you work. Wrap ie cord around the hoop in a loose loop then leave a gap of 5-6cm before rapping it around again. Do this until you have 5 loose loops in total.

se the same length to thread through the first loose loop then move cross to the next loop and so on until you have a second inner layer of ose thread loops.

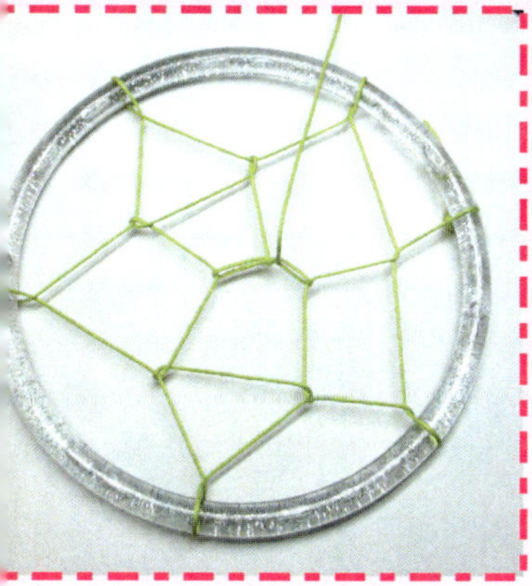

Finally loop the thread around two of the center loops, pull the thread gently upwards, trim to around 12cm and tie a loop on the end ready for hanging the mobile.

Now knot the shoe charms on to the ends of long pieces of nylon cord and add beads to the thread. Loop the thread over one of the cord loops in the center of the hoop to check the length and knot it in place.

he mobile looks most effective when you make lots of beaded strands of iffering lengths and attach them to the cord loops as you go so you can ee the effect as you go. The amount of strands you make is up to you just keep going until you have filled it! Also, if you are uncertain your nots will hold you can always add a tiny dot of glue to the tops to help ecure them.

Top Tip: *If shoes aren't your thing just use different charms or beads that suit your big love!*

Shabby Chic
Fabric Coaster

This is a great way to use up long scraps of fabric and create shabby chic accessories for the home at the same time! The basic technique is very simple and could be adapted to make swirly fabric beads, cushion covers or you could sew thicker fabrics such as denim into rugs. Have fun combining colours, patterns and textures too!

Tools & Materials: Scrap Fabric, Needle & Cotton/Embroidery Thread, Felt

Cut your scraps of fabric into long pieces that are fairly even in width. Lie them on top of each other and use a pin to hold them together.

Begin to plait the strips together, pulling the fabric straight as you work so that the patterned side shows and the edges are tucked into the plait as neatly as possible.

When you get the to the end, trim so that they are all the same length then begin to coil them around, working the length of the plait around the center in coils.

Make a couple of stitches in the end of the coil to hold in place then add the next fabric plait. Continue adding plaits until the coiled piece is as large as you want it to be.

On the underneath of the coil, sew back and forth from the center through the edges of the plait to secure the plaits in place (if working on a large rug you may want to do this as you go).

Check the fabric coil for any rogue fabric edges that may be sticking up and stitch into place neatly if necessary.

To finish off the coaster, cut a circle of felt fabric that is large enough to cover the bottom of the coil. Use several strands of thread or embroidery thread to blanket stitch around the edge.

Top Tip: *Use a thimble to protect your fingers as you stitch the back of the coil!*

Meet the Fluffy Pomlets

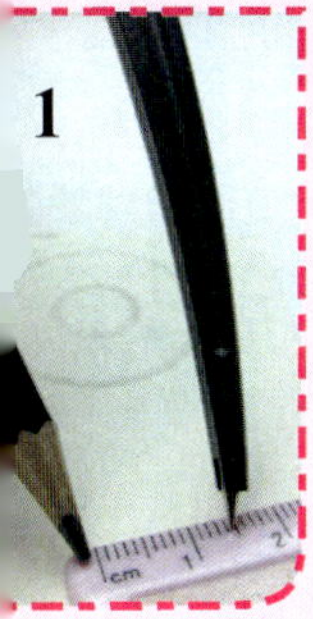
1

I believe that woolly pom-poms are so underrated! These little characters prove that they don't have to just go on woolly hats but can be made into all sorts of things with just a little imagination! These uber-cute flower headed pomlets can be made in all sorts of sizes and shapes with different little hats - better still make a big bunch of them and clip to your bag so they can all jiggle along as you walk!

Tools & Materials: Scissors, Wool & Needle, Smiley People Bead, Honalulu Flower, Bag Charm Finding

ut 2 x circles of scrap cardboard that measure approx. 1.5cm diameter (1). Draw nd cut out a smaller circle in the center of each that measures approx. 0.5cm ameter. Thread a long piece of wool onto the wool needle, hold the two circles gether and thread the wool through the hole, and begin to wind the wool around he cardboard circles through the center hole to the edges. Do this until you can fit ny more wool on (2).

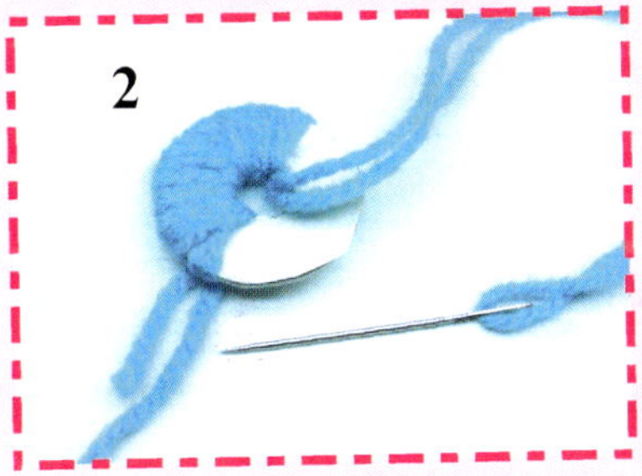
2

3

Use sharp scissors to cut the wool all the way around the edge of the circle (3), making sure to hold the middle so that the wool strands do not come off. Tie a long piece of wool around the gap in between the cardboard circles several times, tightly, then knot it to secure. Leave the ends long.

Cut a slit in each cardboard circle to help you to remove them then 'fluff' up the pom-pom and trim any long ends except the long ends from the middle.

lide a Smiley People Bead and a Honalulu Flower onto the long wool ends (4) and sit them on the pom-om. Separate the two strands, wrap one under the other (5) before threading the end back through the op (6). Continue using the same strand to wrap around the other for a few centimetres until you get a visted cord effect (7). Now just make more 'Pomlets' and attach to the bottom of a bag charm finding!

4

5

6

7

Top Tip: Instead of cute go 'Alien' and add 3 heads to the top of a larger pom-pom!

Delightful
Tin Can Lamp

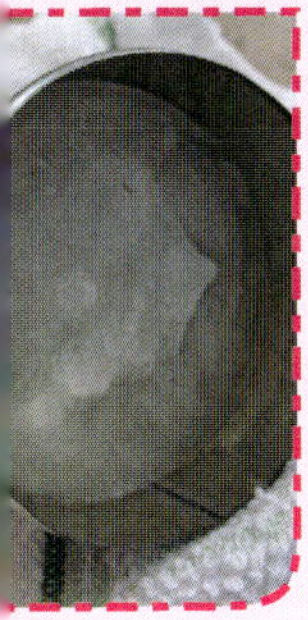

How cool are these?! It's a lovely eco-friendly project with the major bonus being you will actually create lamps that looks fab dotted around the garden and that would make nice little handmade gifts for friends. We are certain you will be wanting to live off baked beans and tinned fruit just so you can get more cans to re-cycle into these little works of art!

Tools & Materials: Tin Can, Wire, Hammer & Nails, Tea Light

The best cans to use for this project are smooth sided although ridged ans can be used - they just make the punching of holes a bit trickier! ou will need a can opener that removes the whole top of the can rather an just the middle of the tops. The edges can be sharp so it's also a ood idea to file off them off with a small metal file (be careful not to stort the shape of the can).

ext you will need to fill the can with water and stand it in the freezer vernight. Only fill to 2cm or so under the rim as the water will expand as it freezes.

When the water is frozen remove the can from the freezer and sit it on a tea-towel on a sturdy surface. At this stage you can either draw on a rough pattern with a felt pen or decide to work freehand. Start at the top of the can and use a hammer to tap large nail into the side to create the pattern holes. The ice will chip under the pressure but your can should stay in shape. Make at least one hole at the top on either side of the can for hanging. You will need to work fairly quickly so that the ice doesn't melt before you have finished your design!

nce you are happy with the pattern, use wire threaded through the two top oles so you can hang the can. Then drop a little hot wax into the bottom of e can to act as glue before putting in a tea light. Light the tea light with a ng handled candle lighter and find a safe space to hang it up where the eat won't cause problems.

Top Tip: *Simple lines of dots look just as effective as a detailed pattern when the can is lit!*

Scrap
Fabric Flowers

Somewhere in that pile of half used fabric bits there are always those that are a little too small to use for much other than patching but are simply too pretty or potentially useful to throw away. Well, this project will have you rooting out all sorts of scraps to work with such as the denim used here because once you know the secret of Scrap Fabric Flower making you will never look back.....

Tools & Materials: Scrap Fabric, Felt, Button, Scissors, Needle & Thread

Draw a circle onto the scrap of fabric - you can use a large glass or base of a bottle. Cut out 2 x circles the same size.

Cut each circle into halves and then half again (so you have 8 x quarter circles). Fold 7 x quarters in half and sew from top to bottom. Turn inside out and with the seams central at the backs , press flat with your fingers to create the 'petals'.

Take a long piece of thread and begin to sew along the bottom curved end of one of the petals, pull the thread as you work to 'ruche' the fabric. Do not fasten off. Add the next petal, making sure the petal seams are facing the back. Continue until seven petals have been sewn onto the same piece of thread. Pull the thread tightly and make a stitch back into the first flower to create a circle of petals. Fasten off.

Cut a circle of felt that is large enough to cover the hole at the back of the flower where all the petals join. Position a button onto the center of the flower and sew to attach it to the felt circle at the back of the flower then sew all the way around the edge of the felt to attach it to the back securely.

Top Tip: *Add a brooch finding or pin to the back or sew them onto bags, hats or make jewellery!*

Skullface
Halloween Light

Make your own spooky little skull tea light covers by using basic beading techniques. In fact... I'd say make lots in all sorts of different stripey combinations (so long as they include black!) and dot all round the garden to add to the atmosphere of All Hallows Eve.... Mwahhh haa hhaa ha!

Tools & Materials: Round Nose Pliers, 28 x 2" Eye Pins, 4mm Round Glass Beads (White, Black, Orange)

tart by threading 11 x 4mm beads onto an eye pin. As you work along the n, alternate black beads with orange beads until you reach just before the nd. Use the tip of the round nose pliers to turn a small loop on end of the wire pproximately the same size as the 'eye' loop). Repeat to make 12 x orange black beaded pins in total & 7 x all black beaded pins.

ow make up the five rows of beaded pins needed to make up the skull pattern y threading the following beads onto eye pins as before as follows:

(1) 4 x black, 2 x white, 5 x black
(2) 4 x black, 4 x white, 3 x black
(3) 3 x black, 5 x white, 3 x black
(4) 3 x black, 1 x white, 1 x black, 1 x white, 1 x black, 1 x white, 3 x black
(5) 3 x black, 5 x white, 3 x black

To assemble the tea light cover begin by threading an eye pin through each loop of 1 x plain back beaded eye pin. Sit them on the eye ends and drop another plain black beaded pin onto one end. Thread another eye pin through its other loop. Repeat until you have a square shape 'stack'.

/ork your way around the stack adding the orange & black beaded eyepins n three sides then the skull pattern rows on the fourth side (in reverse order of ,4,3,2,1). When you get to the top use round nose pliers to coil all the wires into tle 'feet' then turn up the right way and pop a tea light in the middle.

Remember - Do not leave candles unattended!)

Top Tip: Only use beads that can stand the heat rather than ones that will melt!

Embellished Winged Heart

This little padded heart could be stuffed with lavender to scent a room or, minus the ribbon become a cool pin cushion for your sewing box. Pick the fabric and contrasting felt as best befits your colour and mood preference....

Tools & Materials: Fabric, Felt, Wool, Scissors, Needle, Cotton, Soft Toy Filling, Sequins, Seed Beads, Bugle Beads & 3mm Satin Ribbon

old the fabric you have chosen for the heart in half and use the template cut 2 x heart shapes out. Make sure the right sides are together.

ut a length of ribbon that is slightly longer than the heart, double it and ace inside the two pieces of fabric so that there will be a long loop at the p of the heart when the fabric is turned the right way around (leaving the il ends inside).

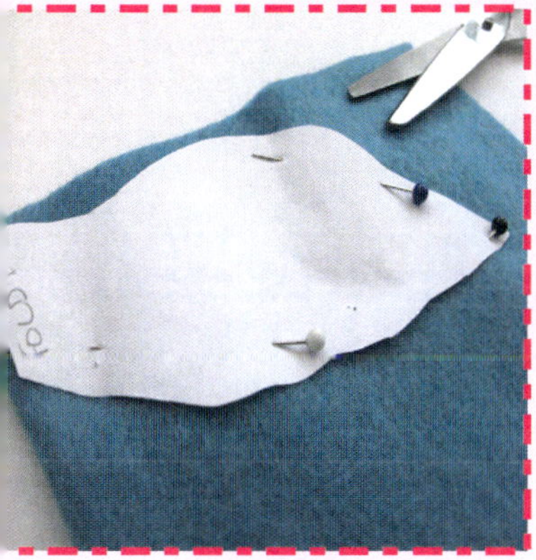

Sew around the heart, leaving a small 2-3cm gap on one side. Turn the whole piece the right way round. Stuff it with some soft toy filling, fold the raw edges inwards and sew the seam neatly together.

Place the wing pattern on the fold of the felt and cut out (x2). Open the first wing shape out fully and sew a pattern onto the fronts of the wings using wool or thread. Embellish with sequins and small beads such as bugle or seed beads.

/hen you have finished decorating the wings, use the second felt wing nape to cover the knots and thread ends at the back - either glue into ace with PVA or sew with small neat stitches that will not show on e front side.

ttach the pair of wings to the back of the stuffed heart with a few stitches o finish!

Top Tip: *Try using plain fabric for the padded heart and embroidering a name on to personalise it*

Patterns Patterns Patterns

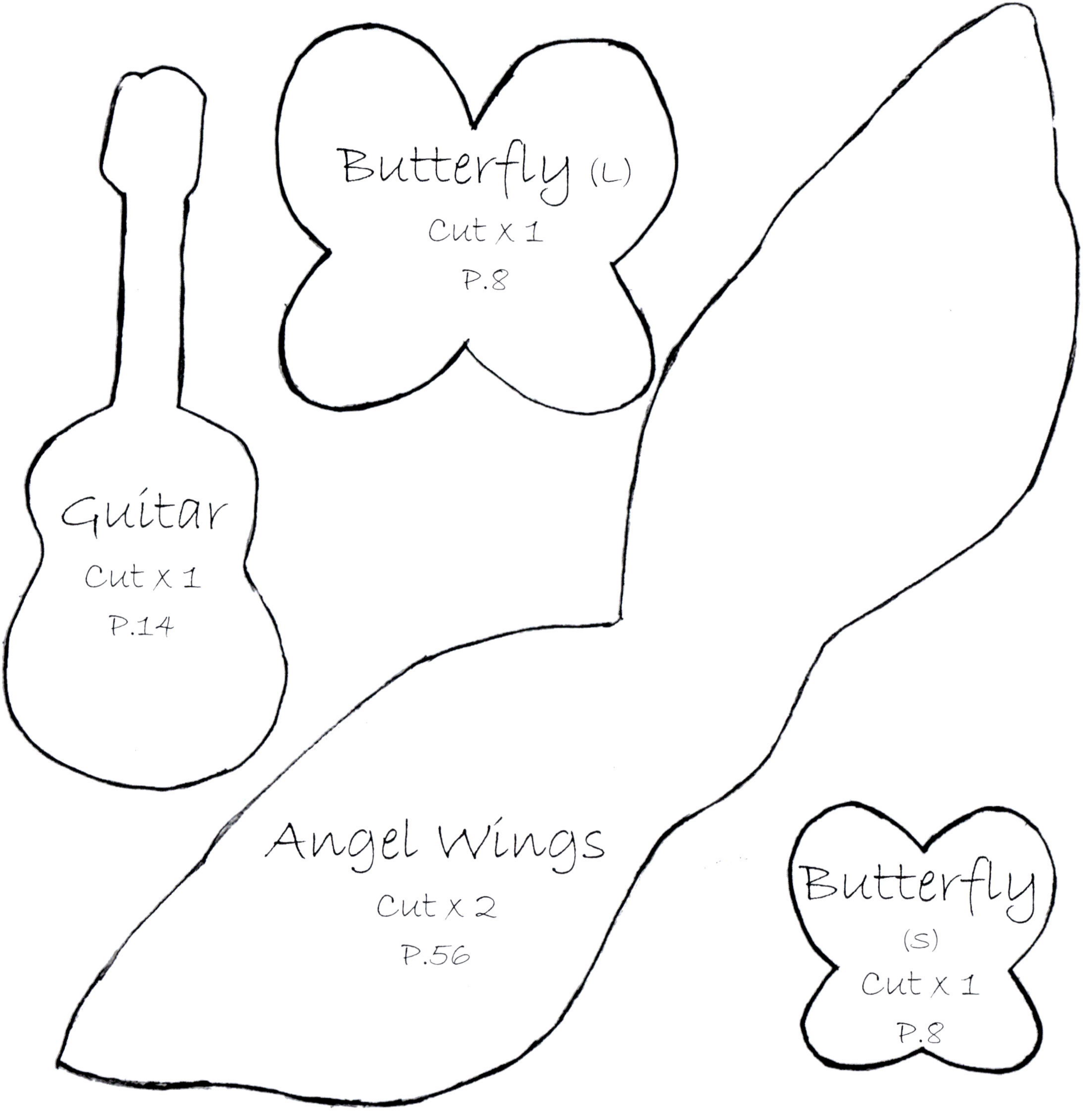